The pool of life

a public health walk in Liverpool

Maggi Morris and John Ashton

Map of Liverpool 1835 CRO

The Liverpool workhouse | The Royal Institution | Irish immigrants

First published in Great Britain, 1997 by
Maggi Morris
Department of Public Health
Whelan Building
Quadrangle
Liverpool L69 3GB

Reprinted 2002

ISBN 0 9529826 0 9

Designed by Text Matters, Reading

Printed and bound in Great Britain by
Biddles Ltd, *www.biddles.co.uk*

NB photograph by Nigel Bruce

CRO image reproduced courtesy of City Record Office

TM photograph by Terry Mealey

Drawing of William Henry Duncan by Fred O'Brien

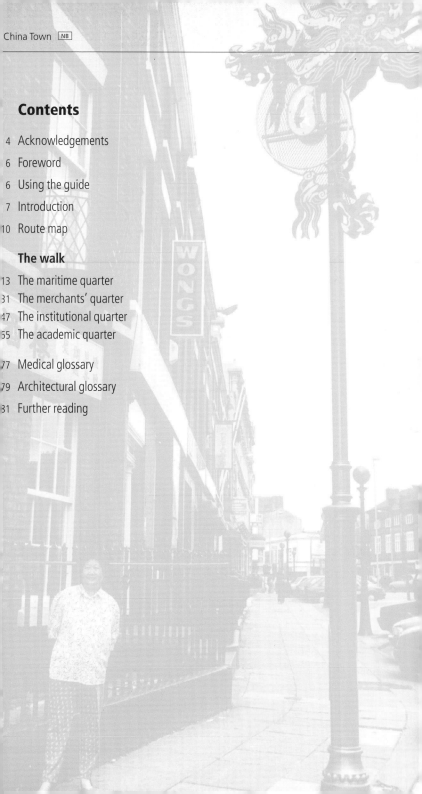

Contents

Acknowledgements

The authors would like to thank the
following people, without whose
advice, assistance and enthusiasm
for such a publication, it might not
have come to fruition:
Adrian Allen, Mike Barber,
Leroy Benons, Simon Biggins,
Philip Browning, Nigel Bruce,
Wendy Cafferty, Philip Davies,
Siobhan Devoy, Tony Fox,
Linda Ferguson, Roger Gray,
Diane Hanley, Quentin Hughes,
Trevor Humphies, Adrian Jarvis,
Dave King, Mary King, Mickey King,
Paul Laxton, Bennet Lee, Corinne Levin,
Lowell Levin, Gillian Mawdsley,
Helena McGourty, Terry Mealey,
Mark Meredith, Kate Parrot,
Peter Pharoah, Mary Jane Platt,
Helen Power, Barbara Robson,
Sally Sheard, Adrian Simmons,
the Sisters of the Missionaries of
Charity, Janet Ubido, John Vaughan,
Colin Wilkinson.

Back-to-back houses CRO

Foreword

This walk has evolved over more than 10 years of providing an orientation to Liverpool and its public health history to a variety of students, but especially to the mature degree students at the Liverpool School of Tropical Medicine and the University of Liverpool Department of Public Health. The stimulus to write it down came in 1991 when Nick Black, from the London School of Hygiene challengingly produced a poster paper of Public Health Walk No.1 *The Victorian Water Supply for London*, for the annual conference of the Society for Social Medicine. By the following year, Public Health Walk No.2 was also in poster format, having been tried out on public health tourists, Lowell and Corinne Levin from Yale University. With the assistance of Gillian Mawdsley, Mary Jane Platt and Helena McGourty and Nigel Bruce (photographs) a *Public health Walk in Liverpool* poster was produced. However, it took the persistance of Maggi Morris with her perspective as a social and architectural historian, and many hours spent in the archive collections, to convert half-truths and guesswork into something more robust.

John Ashton, January 1997

Using the guide

The guide is intended to provide a navigated tour of the past and present social history of public health in a great city. It is not exhaustive, but is intended to be a useful, informative and entertaining account based on the authors' personal perceptions and understandings.

This guide consists of a narrative divided into four quarters, each with a map. The consecutive quarters follow a historical sequence, and also form a progressive walk round the city. If time is short, it is suggested that each quarter is walked on a separate occasion. Interspersed throughout the text are grey boxes of supplementary information to be read in advance or at leisure.

Finally, words written in italics indicate medical and architectural terminology, the technical explanations of which are given in simple terms in glossaries at the end of the walk.

There are many grand buildings in Liverpool and the rules are to look up at façades above street level, to go down side streets to discover hidden architectural gems and to be nosey and put your head inside office doors to appreciate the glory of the private spaces. Above all find somewhere high up such as the Anglican Cathedral tower to get a panoramic view of the city.

Detail from Ear and Eye Infirmary   NB

Introduction

In considering a walk around Liverpool a brief overview of the history of public health since Victorian times is appropriate to set it in context.

Four quite distinct phases of public health can be identified in developed countries over the past 150 years. The first phase began in the industrialised cities of northern Europe in response to the appalling toll of death and disease among the working classes living in abject poverty. The process of urbanisation is conventionally described in terms of 'push' and 'pull' factors. In the British case, much of the population was displaced from the land into the towns and cities by the land owners, wanting to take advantage of the increased agricultural productivity due to more scientific insights into crop rotation and animal husbandry. This coincided with the attraction of growing towns and cities as a result of the industrial revolution and produced a massive change in population patterns and consequently in the physical environments in which people lived.

A predominantly rural way of life was replaced by one in which a seething mass of humanity lived in squalor as industrialisation of urban settings took a firm hold. Over a period of time the response to the associated problems of disease and early death was the development of a locally driven public health movement in which Liverpool was at the forefront.

Liverpool itself was the first town to appoint a medical officer of health, William Henry Duncan (1805–1863) in 1847, taking to heart the recommendation made by Edwin Chadwick (1800–1890) in his general report to the government on the Sanitary Conditions of the labouring population of Great Britain (1842):

'that for the general promotion of the means necessary to prevent disease it would be good economy to appoint a district medical officer independent of private practice, and with the securities of special qualifications and responsibilities to initiate sanitary measures, and reclaim the execution of the law'.

This first phase of public health was driven by the sanitary idea, namely that overcrowding in insanitary conditions was at the root of the epidemics that affected the great towns and cities. It was supported by the first Public Health Act 1848, which emphasised the need to make substantial improvements in sanitation, housing, water, sewerage and the environment.

William Henry Duncan

'A comfortable bed', a sketch by Liverpool district nurse, Lucie Devenish, c1880. COURTESY OF LIVERPOOL CITY LIBRARIES

Towards the end of the 19th century, the sanitary era, having in large measure succeeded in raising environmental standards, gradually gave way to a second phase which developed the idea of personal prevention and a more individualistic approach ushered in by the germ theory of disease. Initially, attention was focused on immunisation and family planning. Later school meals, school and community nursing and social work all began to have a positive impact on health and social welfare. Later still science began to offer real possibilities of therapy in the forms of drugs and surgery. In this third phase, which dates from the 1930s, hospitals and other medical institutions came to dominate the way in which we responded to questions of health.

More recently, during the 1980s and 90s, a fourth phase can be identified with the emergence of the 'new public health' doctrine. It is an approach which brings together environmental improvement with appropriate preventive and therapeutic interventions, especially for the young, elderly and disabled. At the heart of this approach is what is perhaps most appropriately called 'the ecological idea'. This idea goes beyond the mechanical sanitary idea to the recognition that a holistic understanding of humans, their lifestyles, habitats and environments is required to protect both humans and the planet. This new thinking is developing a philosophy of increased public participation, improved integration of different agencies and sectors working together for health, and a re-orientation away from secondary and tertiary hospital care, towards primary and community care, with an emphasis on health promotion.

Through Liverpool's many intriguing streets and alleyways and some of the most notable architecture in Britain, this walk offers some insights into these phases of public health. It also shows Liverpool to be in the forefront of locally driven public health practice, and provides some clues as to the approaches being adopted in the new public health era.

Liverpool's skyline from the Mersey [NB]

The Liverpool Ear and Eye Infirmary [CR]

Sailors' Home, now demolished [CRO]

Town Hall

Dale Street

Water Street

The Strand

James Street

Georges
Pier Head

Mann
Island

Strand Street

Canning Place

Paradise Street

Hanover Street

Gradwe...

Duke Street

Wapping

The
Albert
Dock

Route map

The maritime quarter
••••••••••

The merchants' quarter
– – – – –

The institutional quarter
ooooooooo

The academic quarter
▬ ▬ ▬ ▬

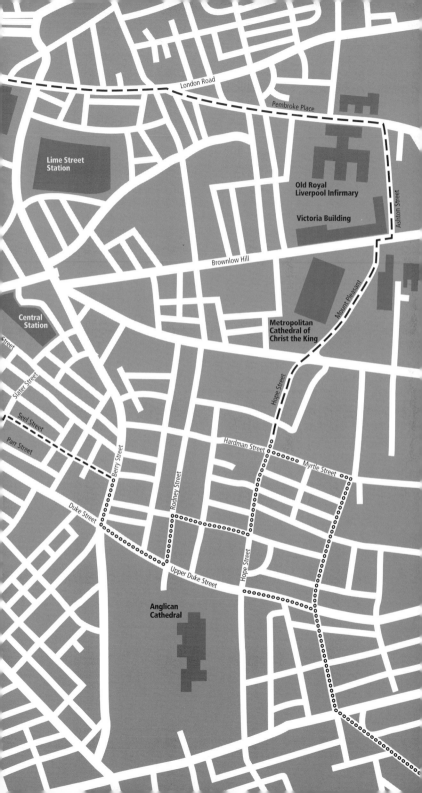

Early view of the Liverpool docks, showing the Church of Our Lady and St Nicholas CRO

The maritime quarter

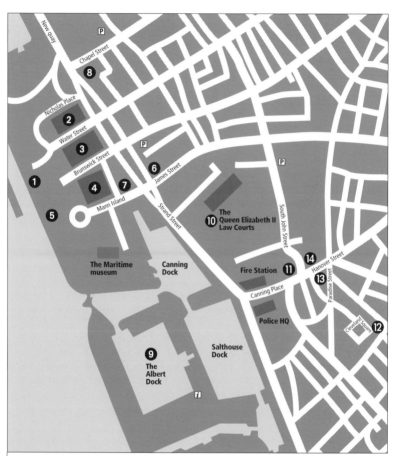

The maritime quarter

1 Pier Head

2 Royal Liver Building

3 The Cunard Building

4 Mersey Docks and Harbour Board Company Building

5 Sir Alfred Jones memorial

6 White Star Shipping building

7 Georges Dock ventilation and control station building

8 Our Lady and St Nicholas Church

9 Albert Dock

10 Chavasse Park

11 Site of Sailors' Home

12 Seamen's Dispensary

13 The Chancery

14 Church House

Map of Liverpool docks 1720 [CRO] Map of Liverpool docks 1835 [CRO]

'With cities it is as with dreams, everything imaginable can be dreamed, but even the most unexpected dream ... conceals a desire or its reverse, a fear. Cities, like dreams, are made of desires and fears, even if the thread of their discourse is secret, their rules are absurd, their perspective deceitful, everything conceals something else'.

Italo Calvino, *Invisible Cities* (1972)

❶ Georges Pier Head

We start at the Pier Head – one of the most well known river frontages in the world, best seen from the ferry boat on the Wirral side of the Mersey. Here one is confronted by the magnificent Liverpool skyline, built on the dreams of wealthy merchants.

During the last century this perspective was indeed deceitful, as it concealed the cramped squalor behind it. Here the city's swelling population (many of whom were Irish refugees fleeing the potato famine of the 1840s) suffered from all manner of social and economic deprivation. Many of the descendants of these refugees stayed in the wards of Vauxhall, Everton and Wapping until their forcible relocation by the City Council in the 1960s and 70s as part of the slum clearance programme.

The Pier Head was also the last sight of Liverpool for some 4.75m Europeans who, in the last half of the 19th century, migrated to North America and Australasia through the port.

❷ Royal Liver Building

Liverpool reached its zenith at the turn of the 20th century, becoming one of the richest cities in the world.

This wealth is vividly expressed in the trio of office buildings erected on reclaimed land at the Pier Head: the Royal Liver Building, the Cunard Building and the Mersey Docks and Harbour Board Building.

The Pier Head group of buildings typifies the money that was spent by those who felt confident that Liverpool was a genuine rival to London. This is also reflected in street names such as Covent Garden, The Temple, Islington and The Strand which echo the streets of the capital.

The left of the three buildings is the Royal Liver Building, designed by Aubrey Thomas and erected between 1908–10. An impressive multi-storey commercial office block, and a tour de force of reinforced concrete frame construction, it is one of the earliest examples of its kind. It is cloaked in stone and fashioned principally in the *Art Nouveau* and *Romanesque* styles, but its grandiose entrance is *Baroque*,

Liverpool's skyline from the Mersey [NB]

Early view of the docks [CRO]

Recent view of the docks [NB]

closely modelled on the ancient Roman Temple of El Deir in Petra, Jordan. The building is the head-quarters of the Royal Liver Insurance Company, which grew out of the Royal Liver Friendly Society (1856), whose origin was a Liverpool burial club established in 1850. Unique to a commercial building is the basement chapel, created during the Second World War as a place for prayer and contemplation.

Inside you can see the refurbished shipping hall with the original stained glass tryptic commissioned by the Furness Shipping Company. The floor is marble, with an inlay design echoing the clockface on the building's towers. In the summer you can take a lift to the top for spectacular views of the Wirral peninsula.

Perched on top of the building's telescoping towers are the famous Liver Birds. It has never been clear what these birds are, but the most popular theory is that they are cormorants up to their knees in mud at the water's edge. Folklore says that when the Birds leave Liverpool the city will be finished. You can see that, during recent economic lean times, they have been tied down to stop them escaping!

❸ The Cunard Building

In the centre, the Cunard Building, designed in 1913–16 by Willink and Thicknesse, appears like a massive merchants' palace of the Italian *Renaissance* dressed in *Greek Revival* detailing. Its grandeur is all the more conspicuous as it was built during the First World War.

It was the headquarters of the Cunard Steamship Company (named after Samuel Cunard, a Canadian who came to Liverpool in 1840 to start a liner service across the North Atlantic). Stepping inside one can still see the impressive Booking Hall and the old Customs Office over the hallway. Both these interiors continue the Greek idiom with some fine architectural design and decoration. Once thronging with customers, these interiors now lie silent and empty, awaiting revival.

❹ Mersey Docks and Harbour Board Company Building

The final piece in this trio, on the right, is the former headquarters of the Mersey Docks and Harbour Board Company (begun in 1858). In the early years of this century the company was trying to impress and attract investors – hence the imposing building.

The funds raised enabled new docks to be developed (such as the Gladstone Docks, begun in 1905) for the ever-larger ships coming into the port.

Pier Head buildings, seen from the river [NB]

The building was completed in 1907 to the *baroque* designs of Arnold Thornley, winner of an architectural competition. A huge rectangular block cleverly conceals large internal lightwells, finished in white glazed tiles, which allow maximum daylight into the offices within.

A detour inside the building reveals a capacious octagonal hall which rises

up to the dome via galleries running around four levels. The details capture a sense of Liverpool's great wealth and association with the sea. Look for the fine metalwork incorporating dolphins, sea horses and shells, and the stained glass windows depicting sailing ships.

The Mersey Docks and Harbour Board Company were keen to look after the health and welfare of the dock workers. During World War Two the company initiated a number of medical centres. These provided workers with free treatment for all but major industrial accidents. They also provided a series of canteens where 'hot and nourishing' meals could be obtained at 'reasonable' prices.

❺ Sir Alfred Jones memorial

The waterfront near the ferry terminal has been recently redeveloped into a piazza by the Merseyside Development Corporation.

Among the memorial monuments, look for the allegorical statue with the relief bust of Sir Alfred Lewis Jones (1845–1905) carved by George Frampton in 1913.

Sir Alfred Lewis Jones CRO

Jones was a ship owner and one of the founders of the Liverpool School of Tropical Medicine (see p73). This first opened its doors to students in 1899, some months ahead of the equivalent London School, and consequently was the first such school in the world.

Lewis also promoted technical education and health services in the West Indies, and was responsible for importing and popularising the banana as a nutritional source of food for the working classes. Previously it had been a rare and exotic fruit consumed mainly by the rich.

Banana cultivation in the West Indies CRO

❻ White Star Shipping building

Move away from the river along Mann Island, named because it was once an artificial island created at the time of Georges Dock (1771) at the Pier Head.

In front of you is the striking office building of the White Star shipping line. Norman Shaw's design of 1898 is in the style of a French castle, with a massive defensive styled ground floor. The alternating horizontal bands of brick and white stone on the façade echo Shaw's similar treatment of New Scotland Yard in London.

The announcement of the sinking of the Titanic was made from the balcony of this building.

❼ Georges Dock ventilation and control station

Behind the Mersey Docks and Harbour Board Building is the Georges Dock building, built to house ventilation machinery and administrative offices for the Mersey (road) tunnel, opened by King George Von 18 July 1934. The two mile tunnel, built to relieve the pressures of increased transport between Birkenhead and Liverpool, is still seen as a great engineering achievement.

This is one of six ventilation shafts which, together with the tunnel ntrances, were designed by one of Liverpool's most notable 20th century architects, Herbert Rowse. This shaft is one of two finished in Portland stone with sculptural relief panels on two elevations, and fine decorative ironwork railings and lamps in a distinctive *art deco* and modernist style.

❸ Our Lady and St Nicholas church

Glimpsed through the angle formed by the ventilation shaft and the Cunard Building is the picturesque Church of Our Lady and St Nicholas, known as the Sailor's Church.

'Am I not a man and a brother?' Slogan of the anti-slavery campaign on a plate NB

Our Lady and St Nicholas church CRO

Nearby once stood the imposing Goree Piazza, a colonnaded warehouse which had tragic associations. Goree was the small island off Senegal where people were mustered before being sold into slavery.

One of the stories you often hear about Liverpool is that slaves were sold here at the river front, and that there were iron rings on the quayside where people were tied up. This is not true. In fact only a handful of Africans were brought to Liverpool in the 18th century, where it was fashionable for captains and merchants to have black children as footmen and pages.

But in this sorry way Liverpool does lay claim to having the oldest black population in Europe – as indeed it

has the oldest Chinese population. The Chinese were pressed to work on ships in China (Shanghaied) – when the ships tied up in the Mersey they ran away and found refuge in the town.

❾ Albert Dock

Towards the Mersey is a panoramic view of the Albert Dock (built 1841–8). From the demise of the docks in the 1960s until the 1980s, this complex lay derelict and under threat of demolition. It has now been restored and is one of the most popular tourist and heritage centres in northern England.

❿ Chavasse Park

Along the Strand and to the left you can see the Anglican Cathedral, and in the foreground the Queen Elizabeth II Law Courts built in 1981.

Cross over to Chavasse Park. This piece of green open space reminds us that the whole area – stretching for several miles in a southerly direction – was originally the Liverpool Moor. Here freemen of the city grazed their sheep. At some point during the 17th century building was allowed on the Moor, so that it was lost.

Chavasse Park however is a hint of the beauty of south Liverpool, which even today is one of the finest suburban areas in the country.

The Albert Dock

The Albert Dock now incorporates the Merseyside Maritime Museum, the Liverpool Tate Gallery designed by Sir James Sterling in 1988, (housing temporary exhibitions of modern art, sculpture and installations), the Beatles Museum, shops, offices and apartments. This transformation of an industrial and commercial environment into a tourist attraction can be likened to that of the London Docks, the Cardiff Docks and even Fisherman's Wharf in San Francisco.

The Maritime Museum includes a new gallery entitled 'Transatlantic Slavery: Against Human Dignity'. (This will at last try to address this neglected part of Liverpool's history and its implications). It also includes the Museum of Migration, which tells the story of migration from Europe through Liverpool in the last century, through an exhibition which involves walking through a reproduction of the kind of vessel that went between Liverpool and New York, and the disembarkation on the other side of the Atlantic to be processed by the immigration authorities of Ellis Island.

This set of buildings has been described as the finest dock architecture in the world. The buildings were fireproof – constructed almost entirely from iron and brick – and were used to store cotton, tobacco and rum from the Americas, all highly inflammable cargoes. The dock complex was designed by the Yorkshire engineer Jessie Hartley (1780–1860), Liverpool's Dock Engineer between 1824 and 1860. Throughout this period he dominated with his personality, technical skills and creative imagination to produce a highly innovative complex of interconnected docks and buildings. After St Katherine's Docks in London, this was one of the earliest examples in the world.

These industrial buildings and dock landscape of brick, cast-iron and cyclopcian stonework, were built 'to endure as long as the Pyramids'. Everywhere can be seen ironwork of capstans, lamp posts, bollards and bridges and the rich texture of the sandstone and granite stonework in the dock basins, steps and walls. The eccentric architectural detailing of the pumphouses, clock towers and watchman's huts add to the visual variety. These docks possess both great utility and architectural appeal, apparent in the confident use of cast-iron Doric colonnades. In the north east corner stands the authoritative cast-iron portico of Philip Hardwick's Dock Traffic Office of 1846, presently the Granada Television Studios.

Ancient Liverpool

The Pier Head buildings, with their references to classical palaces, can be deceptive, for Liverpool isn't really an old city. As an urban environment it is only about 300 years old – a mere adolescent compared with mediterranean cities.

At the time of the Domesday Book the area was occupied by two families. One owned the castle in Castle Street about a quarter of a mile from the river on what is now the site of the Queen Elizabeth II Law Courts and a large statue of Queen Victoria. The castle was demolished in 1721, almost 80 years after the Civil War, when Liverpool had characteristically sided with the Republicans (Roundheads) and had their castle sacked as a punishment.

The other family had the old hall (Vieux Hall) in Old Hall Street where the Liverpool Town Hall, one of the city's oldest and finest buildings, stands today. This is Liverpool's third Town Hall, and dates from a design by John Wood in 1749–54. In 1795 a fire caused serious damage to the building, including Wood's somewhat insipid dome. Extensive rebuilding by James Wyatt included a new and more impressive dome in 1802, and, with the help of John Foster, the Corinthian portico. In 1820 the interiors were extravagantly decorated – recent restoration allows visitors to see the finest late Georgian civic rooms in England.

In the late 17th century, the town began to grow, principally because the River Dee began to silt up. Until that time, the ports of Chester and Parkgate on the Dee had been naval ports, used as bases to maintain English control of Ireland. Now the Navy began to use the River Mersey instead and Liverpool's phenomenal growth began.

Once the naval ships were in the river, other activities followed. First it was used as a base for piracy. As those ships ventured further afield, capturing Spanish galleons and reaching the west coast of Africa, the slave trade grew rapidly. Initially, Bristol and Liverpool competed for this trade, but during the second half of the 18th century Liverpool came to dominate it. The trade was lucrative: jewellery and pottery from the newly emerging industrial towns of Lancashire and the Midlands was shipped to Africa. With it slaves were bought and shipped to the Americas where they were sold. On the return journey the ships carried cotton, tobacco and rum back to Liverpool, guaranteeing the merchant shippers full boats on each leg of this 'triple' passage and generating vast wealth for the owners.

The 'pool'

If you walk along the Strand to the corner of Canning Place, you reach an area where the river estuary once came up to form a pool.

The original Liver-pool went up here to Canning Place, away from the river. There was a very large tributary to the Mersey and the pool itself was the original port of the city.

In 1715 the first wet dock was built by the engineer Thomas Steers, and in 1827 it was filled in and the Fifth Customs House put in its place.

Designed by John Foster in 1812, and begun in 1823, it was at that time Liverpool's largest and most imposing building – and must have seemed all the more so, given the squalor of its immediate neighbourhood.

It was bombed during the war, and, after a period of deterioration, it was demolished and an indifferent office development put in its place – and thus Liverpool lost one of its finest classical buildings.

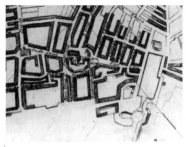

The first wet dock, built in 1715 and shown on a 1720 map (area on right hand side) [CRO]

John Foster, architect of the Customs House [CRO]

Early view of the docks, showing the fifth Custom House building (begun in 1823) [CRO]

Jung's dream of Liverpool

The remnants of the Liver-pool reminds us of the association of Carl Gustav Jung with Liverpool. Jung never visited Liverpool, but in 1927 he had a dream which he recorded and described in his writing:

'I found myself in a dirty sooty city. It was night and winter and dark and raining. I was in Liverpool. With a number of Swiss, say half a dozen, I walked through the dark streets. I had the feeling that we were coming from the harbour and that the real city was actually above on the cliffs. We climbed up there. It reminded me of Basel, where the market is down below and you go up through the Tottengasschen (Alley of the Dead), which leads to a plateau above and to Petersplatz and Peterskirsche. When we reached the plateau, we found a broad square dimly illuminated by street lights into which many streets converged. The various quarters of the city were arranged radially around the square. In the centre was a round pool and in the middle of it a small island. While everything round it was obscured by rain, fog, smoke and dimly lit darkness, the little island blazed with sunlight. On it stood a single tree, a Magnolia in a shower of reddish blossoms; it was as though the tree stood in the sunlight and at the same time was the source of light. The companions commented on the abominable weather and obviously didn't see the tree. They spoke of another Swiss who was living in Liverpool and expressed surprise that he should have settled over here. I was carried away by the beauty of the flowering tree and the sunlit island and thought 'I know very well why he settled here'. Then I awoke.

This dream represented my situation at the time. I can still see the greyish-yellow raincoats glistening with the wetness of the rain. Everything was extremely unpleasant, black and opaque, just as I felt then but I had a vision of an earthly beauty and that is why I was able to live at all.

Liverpool is the 'pool of life'. The Liver according to an old view is the seat of life; that which makes it live.'

The growing population

The most popular theory for the origin of Liverpool's place name is that it came from the 'Liver' or red colour which was produced by reflection of the red Cheshire sandstone bed-rock through the water, before industrial pollution made it one of the most polluted estuaries in Western Europe.

The River Mersey has some 300 miles of tributary which serve a large part of industrial Lancashire and Cheshire. The sanitary theories of the old public health movement encouraged effluents (both human and industrial) to be deposited in the rivers.

With hindsight this can be seen to have been flawed. While it improved the living environment of the industrial working classes of Europe in the last century, nature had little chance of coping with the massive ecological onslaught. This is still true today.

Liverpool's population was still only about a thousand in the 1660s, but doubled every 20 years. By the early 19th century it reached 130,000, rising to some three quarters of a million in the early 20th century. Then economic decline and population loss set in. Nowadays the city has a population of about 460,000 with around 7,000 births a year.

In the first half of the 19th century, Irish refugees moved into the cheap boarding houses and accommodation in the Wapping area, which extends south from here for about half a mile and north along the river bank to the Vauxhall area. The Vauxhall area also became a strong focus for the Irish Catholic population when they began to arrive in the 1840s.

Surrounded by dubious hostels and drinking establishments frequented by sailors, it was said they 'were lucky if they got away with their lives, let alone their purses'. Charles Dickins visited Liverpool on several occasions, and researched this dockland area and the conditions of the sailors. These observations became the basis for his novel 'The Uncommercial Traveller' in which his character, Poor Jack, had to deal each night with the traps set for him by the landsharks. He described the vice and drink that awaited Poor Jack as he came ashore, where he was ill-fed, ill-used and cleaned out. Similar sentiments were echoed in Frazer's 'Duncan of Liverpool'.

'...Several of the neighbouring streets present spectacles of vileness and misery in the lowest forms, from which the heart turns in disgust which almost overpowers the feeling of commiseration. It is deeply to be regretted that dissipation and licentiousness should almost always be the accompaniment of extensive commerce and that valuable character – the British sailor is left to indulgences which destroy the hard-earned wages in orgies of the basest description'. ('A Writer', 1823).

The Sailors' Home, now demolished CRO

⓫ The Sailors' Home

If you turn left into Canning Place, to the right you will see the Anglican Cathedral. 200 yards on the left once stood the Sailors' Home designed by John Cunningham and erected in 1848.

The building was a palatial *Jacobethan* block with corner turrets, echoing the great country houses of Hardwick and Hatfield. It was built with confidence and verve as it dominated the City skyline.

Inside, it was designed to be similar to a ship, with a large central atrium with galleries on all the floors, off which accommodation led. The frontispiece of the Sailors' Home also evokes nautical vessels, with its huge trophies, medallions and ropework encircling the eternal Liver Bird of Liverpool. The carved details of capstans, ropes and pulley blocks were reminders to the nearby chandleries which supplied the great liners when they were working out of Liverpool.

The Sailors' Home, despite protest and to the shame of the City Council, was demolished in 1973, leaving in its place a sunken waste land and some hoardings supported by scaffolding, believed by some to be the last remnants of the Pool.

Front of the Sailors' Home CRO

Inside of the Sailors' Home CRO

⓬ Seamen's Dispensary

Across from this derelict site you can see the old Seamen's Dispensary in Cleveland Square, which was in use up until 1991.

It was housed in what is now the last remnants of an early 19th century residential square, but as the area became less desirable, a public market moved in with a mix of houses, shops and taverns. This is where Chinese immigrants first settled (see p49).

The Seamen's Dispensary NB

⓭ The Chancery

Nearby were two other institutions concerned with the well-being of sailors.

The institutions have now gone, but the buildings remain. On the corner of Hanover and Paradise Street is the building now called the Chancery, which was previously the Gordon Smith Institute for Seamen.

This was founded in 1820 and was the second oldest such institution in England. It aimed to promote the comfort and happiness of seamen and their families with the amenities of home life. It provided accommodation for 300, a library with literature in several languages, and various meeting rooms. The present building dates from 1898 and is characterised by its sweeping curved façade and conspicuous step and volute gables.

⓮ Church House

On the opposite corner of Paradise Street is Church House, originally the Central Institute of the Mersey Mission to Seamen (established in 1854).

The present building dates from 1884 (architect unknown) and is richly ornamented in terracotta and diaper patterned coloured bricks (note the sailing ships). The building provided sleeping, eating and reading accommodation for sailors, and encouraged them to use a savings bank so that they did not squander their money. Since 1956 it has been the offices of the Church of England diocese of Liverpool.

Sexually transmitted diseases

As you can imagine, the Seamen's dispensary was particularly used for venereal disease, which played a very important part in primary health care during the late 18th and 19th century.

The Lock Hospital (see p71), which was located on the Brownlow Hill Infirmary site, was established in 1832 to treat seamen, townsmen and women with venereal diseases. These days treatment is provided by the Royal Liverpool University Hospital.

The maritime connection is still an important consideration in the fight against venereal disease and the contemporary scourge of HIV/AIDS. Liverpool still has shipping links with parts of the world which have high endemic levels of this new disease.

Fortunately to date it seems that the active approach to safe sex and harm reduction has been successful in containing the epidemic on Merseyside.

The Chancery, formerly the Gordon Smith Institute ⊞

The Church House, formerly the Mersey Mission to Seamen ⊞

Prostitution

The Sailors' Home was one of a group of philanthropic institutions founded by merchants and ship owners to provide sailors with healthy and affordable accommodation, hoping to deter them from the drink and the willing arms of 'Jumping Jenny', Mary Ellen or Maggie May, remembered in the famous old Liverpool Folk song:

'Right well do I remember
When I first met Maggie May
She was cruising up and down
Old Canning Place.
She'd a figure so divine
Like a frigate of the line
That me being a sailor I gave chase'

In Liverpool, it was said that 'a young man cannot pass along the street in the evening without meeting with, and being accosted by, women of the town at every step' (Churchman – William Bevan, 1843).

The Victorians saw prostitution as a menace to both moral and physical health, believing that someone could become literally infected with depravity by coming close to the contagion itself. The problem was complicated by the development of the commercial city, whose many streets lay open for all to wander in, and the distinction between 'women of the street' and other women became blurred.

It was acknowledged by some that prostitution was practiced out of economic necessity, and that it did not always represent a life long occupation. Some were indeed 'rescued' and put into domestic service. Characteristically, the Victorians endeavoured to find practical solutions to the problems of prostitution. One solution was to remove middle class women from the city, where the risk was considered highest, up to the safe sanctuary of the surrounding suburban villa houses. Here a woman could be safely engaged in duties of marriage and domestic affairs, and her image of untarnished femininity could pervade.

For working class women, there was no such escape route. The Victorians' typical solution of regularising, by law, physical and moral dangers meant that they suffered the discriminatory and humiliating effects of the Contagious Diseases Acts of 1864, 1866 and 1868. These pernicious pieces of legislation were devised on the pretext of protecting the armed forces and extended over large areas of urbanised Britain, particularly seaports where the risk was considered highest.

The laws empowered the police to take any suspected woman away to be examined by a doctor. If she refused to comply, then she could be imprisoned immediately. Hence all blame, both moral and physical, was placed upon the women, and men were entirely exonerated. It took the determination of Josephine Butler (1828–1906) to eradicate the Acts from the streets and the Statute Books.

Josephine Butler had arrived with her husband from Cheltenham in 1866 so that her husband could take up the headship of Liverpool College for boys. A highly educated woman, whose father had encouraged her learning in areas of social science, she embarked upon her social reforming career with the support of her husband.

In campaigning to have the Acts abolished, she travelled around the country and abroad giving powerful and persuasive speeches. She gained the support not only of the working classes, but also the middle classes who would have normally supported the Acts. She challenged them on the grounds that the Acts were an abuse of civil rights, that they condoned vice and that they openly advertised the double standards of Victorian Britain.

Victory came in 1886 when the Acts were finally abolished. Interestingly, Florence Nightingale (1820–1910), who was very much concerned with the health of the armed forces, saw these Acts as an assault on women and consequently gave her support to their abolition, much to the chagrin of the military and medical fraternity.

Josephine was not afraid to go amongst the poor, and spent time with women in the workhouse making social investigations. She often took prostitutes into her home to help establish them in a new life. She had a passionate belief in proper work training and education for women as a means of achieving womens' suffrage, and in this, she shared much with Florence Nightingale. Both supported the suffrage movement, and regarded their own reforms as equally important as the attainment of the vote.

Josephine Butler plaque, Upper Parliament Street NB

The Royal Institution, c1799 CRO

The merchants' quarter

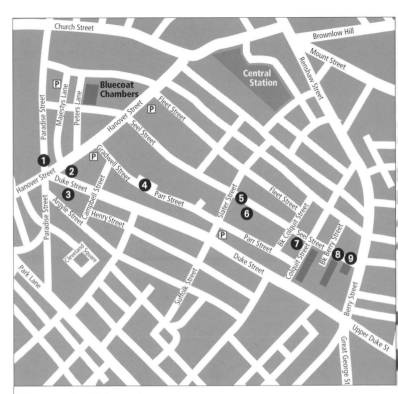

The merchants' quarter

❶ Paradise Street
❷ Hanover Street
❸ Duke Street
❹ Wolstenholme Square
❺ Seel Street
❻ St Peter's Chapel
❼ The Royal Institution
❽ Dukes Terrace
❾ The Blue Angel

❶ Paradise Street

Liverpool is fundamentally a late 18th and 19th century commercial city. However, the corner of Paradise, Hanover and Duke Streets are rather like a gateway from the harbour to a medieval city, distinguished by a circus of round-ended buildings formed by Church House, The Chancery, The Casartelli Brothers Building, and the Headquarters of the Liverpool Housing Trust.

To your left just inside Paradise Street, is a building (now a club) with the statue of an American bald headed eagle on the side.

The Eagle [NB]

This is a reminder of Liverpool's strong connections with America, particularly with the Southern states. American associations included the residence in Liverpool between 1853 and 1858 of the writer Nathaniel Hawthorne (1804–64) who was consul to Britain. Despite his elevated position, Hawthorne seemed to prefer to ramble the streets in order to make his observations about the slum areas of the town, which were in sharp contrast to the merchants' residences, genteel squares and tree-lined promenades that once characterised this quarter.

Another Anglo-American connection is exemplified by the construction in Birkenhead of the Confederate warship *The Alabama*.

❷ Hanover Street

As you turn into Hanover Street you can see, for 200 yards to your right, a substantial row of late 18th century merchants' warehouses with integrated residences. Hanover Street commemorates the connection between the German Hanseatic ports and Liverpool.

❸ Duke Street

Pass into Duke Street on your right. This is the area where the first merchant houses were developed, though it may be difficult to believe this now. Most of the fine, old merchants' houses are now Chinese restaurants, discotheques and clubs. The merchants gradually moved out of the central area under pressure of expanding commercialism.

In order to accommodate increasing numbers of the urban poor, many of these houses became cheap multi-occupancy boarding houses. In fact, one such boarding house just off Duke Street played a part in the later story of the 1849 cholera outbreak in Liverpool (see page 44).

❹ Wolstenholme Square

Turn left through Campbell Street and right into Gradwell Street. This area was once dominated by bustling and noisy warehouses and workshops.

The street leads into Wolstenholme Square, which was once considered an oasis amidst the commercial clamour. Now a shadow of its former self, the square was developed for first class residences.

Here is the earliest example of an enclosed garden for the residents' use, which was formed in an oval shape and laid out with shrubs. The square was only half completed as Duke Street rose in the world and merchants sought residences further away from the river, and the lower end became more commercialised.

Today it is home to the nationally renowned Cream Club, a clue to part of the economic future being created in Liverpool in cultural industries.

Leave the square along Parr Street, named after the banker Thomas Parr, and then turn left into Slater Street. If you look to your right, you will see at the corner of Duke Street what was the Union News Room. This opened in 1801 and was bought by the Corporation, who between 1852–62 established the first public lending library and museum in Liverpool. It is now the headquarters of a local company.

❺ Seel Street

Continue through Slater Street and right into Seel Street, named after Mr Seel who owned much of the land and developed the street over a number of years.

This is one of a group of streets in the south of the inner city where merchants lived in the late 18th and early 19th century. Only when the town became increasingly overcrowded in the mid 19th century, did they move to higher land around Abercromby Square, where the University of Liverpool is now centred.

You can still see the remnants of these Georgian and early Victorian residences with their elegant fenestration and porticoes – sadly some are now in a dilapidated state.

❻ St Peter's Chapel

In Seel Street, about 100 yards to your right, is one of Liverpool's oldest buildings. St Peter's Chapel dates from 1788, making it the oldest Roman Catholic Church in the city.

It was built as part of a Benedictine Mission to provide ecclesiastical accommodation for an expanding Roman Catholic population in the southern end of the town. The simple and unassuming 18th century exterior contrasts with the interior, where 'a glimpse of Italy' may be found. Indeed, the rich *baroque* oratory provided the theatrical setting for the chapel, the once renowned musical services, and in particular, the full orchestral rendering of the Mozart Mass, celebrating the opening of this extension in 1843.

A notable part of the chapel's history was its long established Total Abstinence Society. In 1843, 6,000 signatures were put on a petition in order to secure the series of lectures on total abstinence, to be given by Father Theobold Matthew of Cork. The crowds were such that the service had to be held in the larger church of St. Patrick in Park Road.

In 1938 the Chapel's parish community celebrated its 150 years, and the street was decked from top to bottom with flags and flowers. Today, the street lies quiet, and the chapel now belongs to the Polish Catholic Community.

Opposite the Chapel, where previously the Chapel's presbytery was located, the Benedictine Sisters of the Missionaries of Charity have lived since 1978. They dedicate their lives to looking after both young and elderly women, run a soup kitchen, and work within hospitals, nursing homes, mental institutions and prisons around the Merseyside area.

William Roscoe

❼ The Royal Institution

As you walk along Seel Street you will reach the Liverpool Royal Institution, a rather imposing building on the corner of Colquitt Street.

Originally this was a merchant's house, built c1799 for Thomas Parr, the banker, with counting house and offices forming the side wings and a five storey warehouse behind. It was sold in 1817 and became the home of the Royal Institution. Internal alterations provided a lecture theatre, library and galleries, and the architect, Edmund Aitkin, famous for his essay on the *Doric* Order, provided a new dignified Doric entrance porch.

The Royal Institution was established in 1814 at the instigation of William Roscoe (1753–1831) and his circle, for the 'Promotion of Literature, Science and the Arts'. It provided, from the early 19th century onwards, a setting where major thinkers and scientists of the day were invited to address the local middle classes, giving them a professional and liberal education.

The Royal Institution building is important to the history of Liverpool, as it germinated the seed for the development of the University College for Liverpool (1881), which became the University of Liverpool in 1903.

The Royal Institution building went on to accommodate the University of Liverpool's Department of Extra-Mural Studies, linking the establishment of Liverpool University with its desire to promote liberal education. In an effort to save money, the University sold off the building and thus its ancestor.

In 1834 another important player in the creation of a University at Liverpool also emerged from this historic institution – the Liverpool Royal Institution of Medicine and Surgery.

The Royal Institution building ⬛ NB

Liverpool Royal Institution of Medicine and Surgery

Before the Medical School, no formal medical education was available. Instead lectures were held at the dispensaries, private lessons were given by surgeons, and ongoing training was by the pupillage system.

As early as 1816, the Institution opened its doors for the development of a more coherent series of lectures in surgery, midwifery, and importantly, anatomy. The latter of these was the impetus for the establishment of a Medical School.

William Henry Duncan (see page 40) lectured part-time here, between 1835–1848, and was the School's secretary between 1844–45.

The Royal Institution symbolises a transition in the medical world during the 19th century, from generalist to specialist. The earlier physicians, in common with the 18th century landed aristocracy, had an interest in both liberal arts and natural sciences, and sought to practice in a holistic, non-interventionist and negotiative way with their patients. By contrast the later specialists represented a practice of analysis, specialty, control and bodily intervention.

A view of the Royal Institution c1799 CRO

Teaching anatomy was crucial to a successful medical education. But finding bodies for dissection was difficult – it being a criminal offence to exhume and be in possession of bodies. This may have accounted for the development of ornate iron cages around graves, as rich families protected deceased relatives from this ghoulish activity.

However, it is known that bodies were supplied around Liverpool, with Seel Street a notable location. In 1827 the surgeon William Gill of Seel Street was prosecuted and fined £30 for being in receipt of the exhumed body of Mrs Harrison, who had been buried in Walton church yard, for the purpose of anatomical research. The press described Gill as a 'trafficker' in dead bodies, bringing protests from surgeons who found themselves painted as criminals for pursuing their legitimate and much needed work.

The Royal Institution gave their support to scientific advancement in this area in 1824, when William Rathbone IV called an extraordinary meeting to raise funds to pay fines imposed by the Court on men for raising bodies.

Rathbone pressed for legislation so that unclaimed bodies from prisons, hospitals and workhouses could be used for anatomical purposes. This became the basis of the Anatomy Act of 1832.

The Act prompted riots in the streets around the country. The working class feared their appalling living conditions would be maintained in order to hurry along their demise and therefore provide a plentiful source of bodies. It was also the Act that was to prompt the creation of a fully fledged Medical School at Liverpool.

Between 1834 and 1835 William Gill and Richard Formby presented the first prestigious series of anatomical lectures at the Royal Institution.

❽ Dukes Terrace

On your right, towards the top of Seel Street, via Back Berry Street, is Dukes Terrace. These are the last remaining back-to-back houses in Liverpool, and were only finally vacated in 1974.

This terrace was built on what was previously the gardens of merchants' houses, which fronted onto Seel Street. As the urban population began to press hard on the city centre real fears of civil unrest and imagined fears of moral and physical *miasma* drove the merchants up and out to safer and healthier ground. Their houses were gradually vacated – many of them being used by the incomers for multi-occupancy accommodation.

Back-to-back housing

A hundred years ago Liverpool had tens of thousands of these back-to-back houses arranged in courts. They were put up by speculators to meet the mounting housing demand by the working classes. Greedy landlords and high land prices inevitably forced these houses into multi-occupancy. There would be a cellar room and three further floors, each with one room per floor. The Duke Street example was a row of nine houses and, on the back of them another row of nine. Thus they share the same back wall, and what little light and air there was only reached the front elevation.

In describing this kind of accommodation, Duncan wrote (1844):

'The cellars are ten or twelve feet square; generally flagged – but frequently having only the bare earth for a floor, and sometimes less than six feet in height. There is frequently no window; so that light and air can gain access to the cellars only by the door, the top of which is often not higher than the level of the street.... There is sometimes a back cellar, used as a sleeping apartment, having no direct communication with the external atmosphere, and deriving its scanty supply of light and air solely from the first apartment'.

These conditions were found at their worst in the districts where immigrants lived. Duncan stated that:

'... it is they who will habit the filthiest and worst ventilated courts and cellars; they who congregate most numerously in dirty lodging houses, who are the least clean in their habits and the most apathetic towards everything that befalls them.'

A great worry to middle class Victorians was the considerable risk of diseases spreading among these inhabitants, who lacked any basic sanitation. Together with the overcrowding, the Victorians believed that these houses produced not only an atmosphere of *physical miasma*, but also 'moral miasma', in which sexual improprieties such as prostitution and incest could breed. (Physical miasma was the belief that infectious diseases stemmed from bad air from rotting vegetable and animal matter).

Dukes Terrace back-to-back houses NB

❾ The Blue Angel

Come out of Back Berry Street and turn right into Seel Street.

Look for the Blue Angel Nightclub, the birth place of Duncan. It forms one of a modest line of gentleman's houses developed by the land speculator and builder, William Harvey in 1800. Duncan's father, George, bought the house from him in that year for £800.

Later the Blue Angel became a well known venue for rock bands in the 1960s and is now a popular hang-out for Liverpool Medical Students.

Dr William Henry Duncan

It is in Seel Street that the story of William Henry Duncan – the city and the country's first Medical Officer of Health – begins.

Duncan was born in Seel Street in 1805, the third son and fifth child of George Duncan, a Liverpool merchant. His mother, Christian, was the youngest daughter of the Reverend James Currie of Kirkpatrick Fleming, Dumfriesshire and a sister of Dr James Currie, MD, FRS of Liverpool (1756–1805).

Little is known of Duncan's early life, except that he was educated within the supervision of his paternal uncle, the Reverend Henry Duncan, and that he graduated as Doctor of Medicine at Edinburgh in 1829 with a thesis entitled 'De ventris in reliquuum corpus potestate (on the influence of the abdomen over the body in general)'.

He began his career as a general practitioner. He worked in two dispensaries – one in the south of the town, in Upper Parliament Street, and the other in the north, initially at 12 Marybone but moving to 56 Vauxhall Road in 1831.

Duncan was always interested in the health of the poor, and his concern led him to research the sanitary and housing conditions of his patients and to report upon them – particularly to the Liverpool Literary and Philosophical Society, the major forum for local debate on social issues of the times. (Duncan was also a part-time lecturer at the Liverpool Medical School, 1835–48, and helped establish the Liverpool Medical Society and the Liverpool Medical Institution).

Duncan contested the commonly-held view that Liverpool was a healthy town, because of its commercial prominence. In his pamphlet (1843) on The Physical Causes of the High Mortality Rate in Liverpool, Duncan gave evidence on the conditions under which by far the greater part of the population of the borough lived. Duncan found that typically 25% of his patients were living in cellar dwellings with between 15 and 30 people in an airless room.

His research coincided with the publication in 1842 of Chadwick's Report on an Enquiry into the Sanitary Conditions of the Labouring Population of Great Britain. Among other things this led to the establishment of the Health of Towns Association, inaugurated at a public meeting at Exeter Hall in London on the 11th December 1844.

Duncan and Liverpool were not far behind and a branch was established in the city in April 1845.

The Health of Towns Association

We can get a flavour of the activities of the local Health of Towns Associations by reading the Liverpool Mercury's description of the first Liverpool meeting in April 1845.

The meeting was called by the mayor and attendance was described as "not large but highly respectable", including leading members of the council and both protestant and catholic clergymen, in addition to Dr Duncan and several other members of the medical profession.

The Liverpool Mercury described those present as 'gentlemen of all sects in religion and all parties in politics'. The meeting passed, unanimously, resolutions defining the sanitary objects to be aimed at, and called for legislative action. The duty of the Association was seen to be to 'collect funds, to supply information and to furnish those details which must be the basis of all legislation...' The meeting set up a local committee which published a monthly journal called the 'Liverpool Health of Towns Advocate' for nearly two years; 15,000 copies of the first edition being distributed free of charge.

An important consequence of the activities of the Liverpool Health of Towns Association was the Liverpool Sanatory Act of 1846. In a remarkably short time the collective efforts of these local Health of Towns Associations affected the national political scene, resulting in the 1848 Public Health Act and the development of an effective Victorian public health movement.

One of the early annual general meetings of the Liverpool Health of Towns Association was advertised in the Liverpool Courier by WH Duncan, secretary of the Association. A copy of the front page of the paper carrying the advertisement for the meeting to be held in the Music Hall, Seel Street is to be seen in the gents toilets in the Campanile Hotel on the water front at Wapping. Almost 150 years later in 1986, Liverpool was one of the originating cities in the World health Organisation's *Healthy Cities* initiative, a contemporary parallel.

Sketch of a meeting of the Health of Towns Association, from the
Illustrated London News REPRODUCED COURTESY OF THE TRUSTEE OF THE WELLCOME TRUST, LONDON

Duncan's appointment as Medical Officer of Health

The concern over slum conditions, as revealed by Duncan and Chadwick and the activities of the Health of Towns Association, led to parliamentary action and legislation.

The Liverpool Sanitary Act of 1846 anticipated the National Public Health Acts of 1848 and allowed the city to appoint a Medical Officer of Health. Duncan was appointed, initially part-time with a salary of £300. Within a year his contract was changed to full-time in order to prevent him having a conflict of interest with patients who might, for example, be polluting the streets with their business activities.

The change of contract may have had something to do with a sarcastic piece in an early edition of Punch – see opposite.

Thus at an early stage the principle was established that advocates of the city's health should be independent of outside influences.

This unfettered right to place matters on the political agenda has continued until the present, with interruption (1974–88).

Perhaps equally important was the tradition which began with Duncan and his peers, such as the Borough Engineer, James Newlands and the Sanitary Inspector, Thomas Fresh, of reporting annually on the health of the populace to the Health Committee.

William Henry Duncan

Article from *Punch*, 1847 XII, 44

THE VALUE OF HEALTH AT LIVERPOOL.

By the papers *Mr. Punch* learns that the Town Council of Liverpool intend to appoint an Officer of Health, whose duties will consist in the direction of their sanatory arrangements, and whose services they propose to remunerate by a salary of £300 a year, with the liberty to augment that handsome income, if he can, by private practice.

Mr. Punch will engage to find a competent person, who will willingly undertake the responsibilities of this office, on the liberal terms proposed by the Town Council of Liverpool.

Mr. Punch, on behalf of the respectable medical gentleman, his nominee, will promise that he, the said respectable medical gentleman, shall devote his full attention to his official duties, and endeavour to make money by private practice only at those few leisure moments when he shall have nothing else to do. For, although a practitioner of any eminence expects, generally, to make at least a thousand a year, this gentleman shall regard his situation, bringing him in £300, as of primary importance, and shall look upon his private earnings as matters of secondary consideration.

If the Officer of Health recommended by *Mr. Punch* shall have for a patient a rich butcher, with a slaughterhouse in a populous neighbourhood ; an opulent fellmonger or tallow-chandler, with a yard or manufactory in the heart of the town, he shall not hesitate from motives of interest to denounce their respective establishments as nuisances. He shall not fail to point out the insalubrity of any gasworks, similarly situated, the family of whose proprietor he may attend ; and if any wealthy old lady who may be in the habit of consulting him shall infringe the Drainage Act, he shall not fail to declare the circumstance to the authorities.

Mr. Punch repeats, that he will pledge himself to produce an able and experienced medical practitioner, who shall fulfil all these conditions ; but he respectfully asks the Town Council of Liverpool who, but himself, would for a moment encourage them to expect such a man —for their money.

The Asiatic cholera outbreak of 1849

Throughout the 1840s a stream of Irish refugees arrived in Liverpool, fleeing from the potato famine caused by blight. The stream became a flood in 1847 when, by the end of June;

> 'not less than 300,000 had landed in Liverpool. Of these it was very moderately estimated that from 60,000 to 80,000 had located themselves amongst us, occupying every nook and cranny of the already overcrowded lodging-houses and forcing their ways into the cellars which had been closed under the provisions of the Health Act of 1842. In different parts of Liverpool 50 or 60 of these destitute people were found in a house containing three or four small rooms, about 12 feet by 10; and in more than one instance upwards of 40 were found sleeping in a cellar'.

Duncan, like his uncle, Dr James Currie before him, recognised that profound poverty, unemployment and poor housing could be associated with diseases such as typhus. *Typhus* was known as the Irish Disease on account of an outbreak at the height of Irish immigration into Liverpool in 1847 when it claimed some 5,845 lives.

Duncan repeatedly drew attention to the dire situation, and warned of a likely catastrophe. His words were not long in coming true. In 1848 the *Asiatic Cholera* struck Liverpool.

The cholera had entered Europe on previous occasions. This time it came to Liverpool by way of Glasgow and Dumfries. On 10 December 1848 an Irish family arrived in Liverpool by steamer from Dumfries, where the epidemic was at its height. On landing one of the children was found to be suffering from cholera and both parents went down with the disease on the night of their arrival in Liverpool.

All three died, and on the 15th a woman residing in the same house who had washed the bodies and bed clothes of the deceased died after twelve hours' illness. The first case of undoubted Liverpool origin occurred on the 16th in a crowded house in Back Portland Street in the Vauxhall area. The victim was a girl about 14 years of age.

By the summer of 1849 several hundred people were dying each week, and 'In Lace Street, one third of the ordinary population of several hundred persons died in the course of the year' Frazer, p58.

The 1849 epidemic burned itself out, and when cholera returned in 1854 its impact on Liverpool was much less. The extent to which this was the result of the activities of Duncan and his aptly-named sanitary inspector Thomas Fresh, is open to question. They believed that epidemics were caused by the *miasma* – the bad air caused by rotting animal and vegetable matter. They energetically applied the theories of the time – such as closing cellar dwellings and lime-washing affected houses – but they were working to a faulty theory. It was still more than 20 years before the *germ theory* of disease was identified by the Pasteurs in France. Ironically many of the measures that were taken – such as ventilation and simple disinfection – were probably doing some of the right things for the wrong reason.

19th century Irish migrants to Liverpool CRO

The Liverpool Eye and Ear Infirmary CRO

The institutional quarter

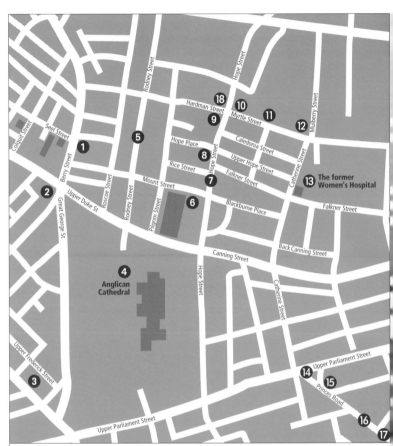

The institutional quarter

1. Berry Street
2. China Town
3. Upper Frederick Street
4. Anglican Cathedral
5. Rodney Street (Duncan's family house no.54)
6. Liverpool Institute for Performing Arts (LIPA) formally Liverpool Institute for Boys
7. Hope Street
8. Hahnemann Homoeopathic Hospital and Dispensary
9. Blind Institute
10. Josephine Butler Building
11. Ear and Eye Infirmary
12. Myrtle Street Children's Hospital
13. The former Women's Hospital
14. Florence Nightingale Memorial
15. District Nursing Home
16. Institute for the Deaf and Dumb
17. Josephine Butler Training House
18. Philharmonic Hotel

Cleveland Square CRO

Moving away from the merchants' quarter there is a sense of transition from the first sanitary phase of public health, into the phase of personal preventative measures. It was the establishment of an infrastructure in the shape of washhouses and clinics and later, organised personal health services and institutions, which marked the later decades of the 19th century.

❶ Berry Street

At the top of Seel Street is Berry Street. From here you can look across to the Blackie, formerly the Congregational Chapel, Great George Street, designed between 1840–1 by J Franklin. This is now a community Arts Project for inner city children.

❷ China Town

Beyond the Blackie is China Town. It is the oldest China Town in Europe, but not the largest, having a population of only about 10,000.

❸ Upper Frederick Street

Off the far end of Great George Street is the site of the world's first public washhouse in Upper Frederick Street. It was opened on 28 May 1842.

The external appearance was reminiscent of a methodist chapel with its simple triangular pedimented façade. However, the lunette windows (semicircular in shape) echoed those found in the Dioclecion baths of ancient Rome.

Inside the Methodist theme continued with the use of galleries on the first floor. The plan included not only bath and washing facilities, but a washhouse for infected clothes, a waiting room and parlour for socialisation, and a reading room.

| The Blackie NB

China Town NB

Upper Frederick Street washhouse, now demolished CRO

Washhouses

The baths and washhouse movement of the mid-nineteenth century was an expression of concern for the cleanliness of the poor, in order to protect the middle and upper classes from disease. The poor were considered a 'dangerous class', not least because they were considered unclean on account of their dirty bodies and clothing. This in turn raised fears about their ability to spread disease.

Public baths did exist earlier, but primarily for pleasure, and thus the poor had little or no facilities for washing and laundering. Liverpool pioneered public services for bathing and washing. The first facility for the poor to wash their clothing appeared in 1832 in the house of Catherine Wilkinson (1786–1860), a poor but hard working, highly religious woman, who came over from Ireland in 1812. She allowed her neighbours to wash their clothes in her back kitchen during the cholera epidemic of 1832.

Her initiative was supported by William Rathbone, who employed her husband as a porter in one of his warehouses in Liverpool, and it was Kitty and her husband, Thomas, who were the first superintendents to the Upper Frederick Street Public washhouse. Rathbone's motives were no doubt altruistic but the corporation's desire to make money ultimately made the washhouses too expensive for the poor, and the installation of a vapour bath at Frederick Street in 1848 indicated that the cleanliness of the poor was not their primary concern. Despite this, Liverpool was seen as a model for the baths and washhouse movement and the Bath and Wash House Acts of 1846 and 1847 enabling municipal corporations to construct them in their towns was acknowledgement of the perceived success in Liverpool. The plan included not only bath and washing facilities but also a waiting room and parlour for socialising and a reading room.

The reading room reflected the earlier activities of Kitty, who had given literacy classes to her neighbours. Its inclusion extended the concept of health beyond personal hygiene as a means of disease prevention to that of education for better self prospects.

Kitty's portrait was to be found in all the subsequent bath and washhouses erected throughout Liverpool, and she was presented with a silver teapot at a ceremony at Mossley Hill (now Carnatic Hall), when she retired in 1853.

Kitty died at the age of 73, and was buried in St. James' cemetery behind the Anglican Cathedral, where she is remembered in the stained glass window of Liverpool's noble women in the Lady Chapel. Upper Frederick Street washhouse was damaged during the May 1941 Blitz and restored afterwards, but unfortunately didn't survive the planners in the 1960s and was demolished. It reminds us of several other Liverpool firsts which include community nursing, school nursing (both started by the Rathbone family) and the first infant feeding station providing supplementary feeds to nursing mothers (begun by Dr Stallybrass).

tained glass portrait of Kitty Wilkinson
the Anglican Cathedral NB

Upper Frederick Street washhouse,
now demolished CRO

❹ Anglican Cathedral

As you pass along Upper Duke Street, to your right is the Anglican Cathedral dramatically situated on St James' Mount. It surveys the city on one side and St James' Cemetery on the other.

The Cathedral was built as a result of the diocese of Liverpool being created in 1880 and, consequently, Liverpool becoming a city. One of the largest cathedrals in Europe, it was designed by Giles Gilbert Scott as a result of an architectural competition. It was started in 1902 and continued to be built until quite recently.

The decision to build such a conspicuous pile has not always met with praise. A poem by Sir William Watson highlights the disparity between the sense of great wealth and well-being signified in such a project, and the poverty and deprivation experienced by so many in Liverpool.

'City of festering streets by Misery tro

Where half fed, half clad children swarm unshod

While thou dost rear that splendid fane to God.

Oh rich in fruit and grains and oils and ores

And all things that the feastful Earth outpours,

Yet lacks leechcraft for those leprous stores ...

Let nave and transepts rest a while; but when

Thou hast done His work who lived and died for men,

Then build his temple on high – not, not, till then'

Sir William Watson (1858–1935) 'Thoughts on Revisiting a Centre of Commerce'.

❺ Rodney Street and Dr Duncan's house

Beyond Roscoe Street and to your left is Rodney Street, the fashionable late 18th and early 19th century street developed for the professional classes

Rodney Street NB

The four times Prime Minister William Gladstone was born at number 62 in 1809. Liverpool's doctors were said to have chosen this elegant street and 'made it their own'. Duncan and his family lived at number 54 in the 1840s, and the Liverpool Childrens Hospital moved to number 58, where it admitted in-patients for the first time.

Today, Rodney Street remains visually pristine with its array of ironwork balconies, fan windows and portico designs, and is still inhabited by private consulting rooms.

❻ Liverpool Institute for Performing Arts (LIPA), formerly Liverpool Institute for Boys

Turn right up Mount Street, where you can glimpse the silvered dome of the Catholic Church of St Philip Neri.

On your right is the imposing Ionic portico of the former Liverpool Institute for Boys. Originally it was the Mechanics Institute of 1835–37, and now, after refurbishment by Brock Carmichael architects, is the newly opened Liverpool Institute for the Performing Arts. This is an initiative of the famous Beatle, Paul McCartney, who went to school there. LIPA activities include using arts in health promotion work.

❼ Hope Street

On reaching the top of Mount Street, we arrive in Hope Street, with its many associations of the 18th and 19th century Liverpool.

Notable is the former Liverpool Institute for Girls, Blackburne House, once the private residential home of James Blackburne (Lord Major of Liverpool). Blackburne House dates from the late 18th century, and was enlarged in the 19th century.

It recently re-opened after extensive architectural refurbishment by Pickles Martinez Architects, as the Women's Technology Scheme. Both initiatives are examples of active urban regeneration in Liverpool.

❽ Hahnemann Homoeopathic Hospital and Dispensary

Hope Street was considered to be situated on the highest and healthiest land of the city, and was therefore a suitable site for the Hahnemann Homoeopathic Hospital and Dispensary which opened in 1887. The building is now part of Liverpool John Moores University.

Hahnemann Homoeopathic Hospital NB

Homoeopathy was not, at the time, recognised by the medical establishment, and it was not until 1923 that the Liverpool Medical Institution (see p67) finally accepted homoeopathic practitioners as members.

The rich sugar merchant, Henry Tate, inspired by personal experience, provided the initial cost of £13,000 for a hospital of 50 beds. Tate was a subscriber to the Royal Infirmary, situated not far away, which was being built at the same time. As with the Royal Infirmary, advice from Florence Nightingale was used to provide guidelines for this building.

Designed by AH Holme in the French *baroque* style, its bright appearance is due to red Ruabon brick facing with white stone *quoins*, *string courses* and window dressings. Inside, the walls were treated in glazed brick, making them fire proof, easy to clean and hygienic in appearance. The basement had several uses, acting as a mortuary, a wine and beer cellar, dispensary and consulting and waiting room.

A hydraulic lift for patients forms the centrepiece, and its iron doors with HH incorporated in them still exist today. Large south facing bay windows characterised the building and gave much light and ventilation to the wards. Much attention was given to ventilation and heating and the self-acting suction power principal designed by Doctors Drysdale and Hayward of Liverpool was implemented. The system was also used in several houses in the area, including the house of Dr Hayward at Grove Street.

This house (1867) is now known as the Octagon (on account of the octagon shaped bay window tower).

Hayward was a doctor who was convinced that good thermal comfort was linked to good health. In 1872 he wrote a book entitled 'Health and Comfort in House Building'.

His house was unique in being designed throughout to provide a tight environmental control system. One sign of this is the unusually tall chimney to extract air. Today, concerns about cold, damp, poorly heated and ventilated housing still preoccupy housing and health agencies.

Twenty yards nudging into Hope Place is the portico entrance to the Homoeopathic Hospital Dispensary.

❾ Blind Institute

On reaching Hardman Street, on the right hand corner is the Philharmonic Hall, recently refurbished by Brock Carmichael Architects. To the left is the Blind Institute, designed in 1851 by AH Holme, and extended in 1931.

It is a mid-nineteenth century classical building, distinguished by its projecting curved pavilions either side of the entrance. Behind the façade, the main central corridor reached a crossing leading to two rear wings.

Back view of Hahnemann Homoeopathic Hospital NB

The 1931 Hope Street extension was designed by Minosprio and Spencely in a *Greek revival* style then fashionable in America and Liverpool. It housed workshops and a shop and was constructed on the site of a former chapel of the Blessed Virgin. This was previously on Great Nelson Street, but moved in 1851 to Hardman Street. A reminder of this is to be found over the doorway in Hope Street:

Christ heals the blind for
Who denighs that in the mind
Dwell truer sight and clearer
Light than in the eyes.

The lean classical temple like building was once enlivened by a pair of doors designed by James Woodford (1893–1976) with relief panels depicting the occupations of inhabitants and the New Testament scene of Christ healing the blind. These doors are now located in the school's premises in Wavertree. Relief sculpture can be seen at the *architrave* level around the extension alluding to some of the talents that Pudsey Dawson endeavoured to promote in the schools, such as basket-weaving and music-making.

The building is now the home of Merseyside Trade Union and Unemployment Resource Centre.

Pudsey Dawson, founder of the Liverpool School for the Blind CRO

On the opposite corner of Hardman Street and Hope Street is the Philharmonic Hotel – a good place to rest!

But first it is worth an excursion along Myrtle Street to capture the richness of the specialist hospital building era.

The rich collection of hospitals in this area reflects the period of growing specialisation of medical treatment beginning in the late Victorian age. This only ended in the 1970s, with the rationalisation and concentration of hospitals onto a few sites and the

Edward Rushton, a founder of the School for the Blind

In 1790 one of Liverpool's merchants, Edward Rushton (1746–1814), a founder of the School for the Blind, contracted ophthalmia on a slave ship to the West Indies, and was left permanently blind. It is thought that he had selflessly put himself amongst the sick slaves.

His experiences had two notable outcomes. Firstly, he became an active abolitionist and writer of anti-slave poetry. Secondly, having met with several other fellow members of the Literary and Philosophical Society to discuss the establishment of a blind fund, he helped set up the first ever school for the indigent blind, which opened in 1790 in Commutation Row.

The ultimate founder of the School was Mr Pudsey Dawson, who established the philosophy of the school in which the many talents of the blind were recognised. Thus the school gave blind persons education, occupational training and support. Nowadays, such ideas seem commonplace, but in the days of Rushton and Dawson it was a new approach to dealing with those with incurable conditions.

Murals

Over the crossing in the old Blind Institute is a dome recently painted by Mike Jones, who established himself as an artist of Trade Union murals. This mural was commissioned by the Merseyside Trade Union and Unemployment Resource Centre, to demonstrate the radical history of the building's occupants. Depicted on the ceiling is Rushton blindfolded with his arm around a black boy on board ship; originally he was to have painted a slave ship, but this was considered too controversial. The second theme depicts the march for jobs in 1980 between Liverpool and London, one of the outcomes of which was the setting up of the Unemployment Resource Centre.

Also depicted is the overhead railway with dockers meeting underneath, remembered still by so many Liverpudlians which ran from Seaforth and the North Docklands to Dingle in the south. In 1979, the Tate & Lyle sugar refinery closed down, leaving the area around the north docks devastatingly depleted of employment. Today, the area is still marked by large scale unemployment. But out of this, new hopes of urban regeneration have emerged as the Eldonian Housing Initiative shows, and the mural depicts such hopes against a crumbling refinery building.

| Murals REPRODUCED BY KIND PERMISSION OF THE MERSEYSIDE TRADE UNION AND UNEMPLOYMENT RESOURCE CENTRE

beginnings of the revival of primary medical care. The development of hospitals during the 19th century helped bring about greater access for the ordinary person to hospital care.

❿ Josephine Butler Building

Situated on the far corner of Hope Street and Myrtle Street is the Josephine Butler Building, designed by Culshaw and Sumner in 1867.

This was the original cancer and skin disease hospital, later the Radium Institute. It now houses the Liverpool John Moores University School of Law, Social Work and Social Policy. It is a reminder of the pioneering role Josephine Butler played in developing social welfare in Liverpool.

Josephine Butler Building　NB

⓫ Ear and Eye Infirmary

Further along Myrtle Street on the same side was the Ear and Eye Infirmary (now part of the City of Liverpool Community College).

This grew out of two institutions: the Opthalmic Infirmary, established in 1820 at the corner of Wood Street and Slater Street, and the Ear Institute. They united in 1841. It was only in 1927 that services for larynx and throat were provided.

Initially they were based in Harford Street, then Mount Pleasant, before moving to these specially-designed premises, built by GO Ellison and Son, winners of a competition.

The building is in the domestic revival style, complete with oriel and dormer windows. Above the entrance is a terracotta relief sculpture depicting Christ healing the blind. Large bay windows reflect a concern for large airy and light interiors to prevent cross-infections in wards and provide good observational light.

Further along Myrtle Street was the Children's Hospital and Maternity Hospital. Opposite this was the home for Destitute Children.

Ear and Eye Infirmary　NB

⑫ Myrtle Street Children's Hospital

During the first half of the 19th century, there were only a scattering of children's dispensaries to deal specifically with children's illnesses. During the 1840s English medical journals were critical of the ignorance about children's diseases and tried to promote a more informed paediatric medicine in the form of children's hospitals. Such hospitals were already to be found in Paris and other European cities, but the English were slow to respond.

The reasons given for this reluctance included the claim that children's hospitals would become dumping grounds for irresponsible parents, and the citing of high mortality rates experienced by the French on account of poor nurse training and the admission of children with infectious diseases. However the Chadwick Report of 1842, and those of the Health of Towns Associations in 1844 and 1845, made it clear that the living conditions of the labouring poor were unfit to deal with the care of sick children.

The Liverpool Infirmary for Children (as it was originally called) was founded in 1858 in Rodney Street. The present building in Myrtle Street was erected in 1866–67, with later extensions. In 1920 the Infirmary amalgamated with the Royal Liverpool Country Hospital for Children at Heswall, Wirral (founded in 1899 by Sir Robert Jones, the pioneering orthopaedic surgeon, and others) to form the Royal Liverpool Children's Hospital. The Heswall branch closed in 1985.

The Myrtle Street Children's Hospital pioneered educational facilities for children in hospital. In recent years it has been run jointly with Alder Hey Children's Hospital, a few miles away in the suburbs of West Derby.

Myrtle Street has for a long time provided primary paediatric health care to families in deprived areas of central Liverpool. More recently it has been replaced by a paediatric resource and health promotion centre as Liverpool's institutions adapt and change to tackle the modern 'new public health problems'.

⑬ The former Women's hospital

The former Maternity Hospital in Oxford Street dates from 1924–26, but the first obstetric and gynaecological hospital in Liverpool was established in 1841, eventually moving to this site.

Amongst the pioneers associated with this hospital was Dr RJ Minnitt who first introduced his 'gas and air' analgesic machine. This hospital has now closed down and has been relocated in the New Women's Hospital.

Turning right to reach Catharine Street we enter into one of Liverpool's best preserved early Victorian residential areas. Here is the former Liverpool Women's Hospital, now student apartments.

This building dates from 1926–32, but its origins date back to 1796 when the Ladies Charity was established in School Lane.

In 1869 the Charity amalgamated into the separate lying-in Hospital and Dispensary for the Diseases of Women and Children which had been established in 1841.

In 1995 this hospital, together with the Liverpool Maternity Hospital and Mill Road Maternity Hospital, transferred to a new hospital in Upper Parliament Street. This latest initiative is considered forward-thinking, as it has encouraged women in the local community and hospital staff to influence the development of the women's hospital. The architect, Jane Lock-Smith of HLM Architects, has also stressed the amount of community consultation that has taken place in the design process.

The new Women's Hospital NB

⑭ Florence Nightingale Memorial

On the corner of Upper Parliament Street and Princes Road the story of community nursing begins.

The main players are remembered in the Florence Nightingale (1820–1910) Memorial, set into the boundary wall. Behind are the former premises of the Liverpool Queen Victoria District Nursing Association, which grew out of the community nursing initiative.

The monument was sculpted by ⧫ Alan to the designs of the firm of Willink & Thicknesse. Executed in granite, the central relief panel shows a typical rendering of Florence as the 'Lady with the Lamp', attending wounded soldiers.

Florence Nightingale CRO

Florence Nightingale memorial, Upper Parliament Street

RIAL WAS
1913 BY
IVERPOOL
IDE TO
NCE
GALE.
NG OF
NDAUNT
TIES SHE
OUR TO
OUNDED
EA AND
NATIONS
FERING.
REDEEM·
Y AND

·EACE
· AND
· WON
·ATION
PLACE
N ·'HE

FLORENCE
NIGHTINGALE
1820-1910

This is set into a temple frame, flanked by wall seats and tablet inscriptions, commemorating the important relationship between Florence Nightingale and Liverpool. This relationship resulted in a number of pioneering public health initiatives with William Rathbone, which had national consequences.

⓯ District Nursing Home

The establishment of trained nurses to nurse people in their own homes was the idea of William Rathbone – see page 62.

In 1897 the city decided that funds raised in commemorating Queen Victoria's long reign, together with financial assistance from the David Lewis Trust, should be put towards the expansion of the district nurses' work. This resulted in the formation of the Liverpool Queen Victoria District Nursing Association. This is recorded on the stone carved parapet.

⓰ Institute for the Deaf and Dumb

Along Princes Road is the Institute for the Deaf and Dumb. Built in 1887, this red brick and terracotta building has an unusual octagonal design. The upper half was used for church services.

⓱ Josephine Butler Training House

Number 15 Princes Avenue is the Josephine Butler training home which opened in 1920 to train people in social work for vulnerable mothers. Here students learnt about physiology, psychology, legal aspects of the work, hygiene and domestic economy.

Thus it reflected the work that Josephine had pioneered in Liverpool.

⓲ Philharmonic Hotel

To end this section of the walk, you can return to the Philharmonic Hotel, designed in 1898 by Walter Thomas, an established brewery architect.

Here one experiences the rich and intoxicating ensemble of architecture and interior design of the fin de siecle. Make sure to pay a visit to the gentlemen's lavatories, featuring rose coloured 'pissoirs'.

Institute for the Deaf and Dumb NB

The story of community nursing

When William Rathbone's wife became chronically ill, she was nursed privately in her own home by Mary Robinson. When she died in 1859, Rathbone was determined to provide such care for all in the community, not just for those who could afford it.

He sought Florence Nightingale's advice on setting up a district nursing service to provide, for the first time, skilled nursing care in the homes of the poor.

He knew that Florence had already developed ideas on this. She believed the training of a community nurse went beyond that of a hospital nurse's training. Community nurses, as well as attending the sick, would need to advise whole families on care, sanitation and health promotion, and this advice should be given with 'kindness and consideration'.

Florence's environmental attitude to health management no doubt arose because she was well aware of the serious consequences to health of urban working class housing conditions.

In 1859, at his own expense, Rathbone established the District Nursing Service. For this purpose Liverpool was divided into numbered districts, hence the term 'District Nurse'.

Florence advised that nurses be trained at the Royal Infirmary and a proportion syphoned off to community nursing. In 1862 therefore William Rathbone funded the erection of the building to house the Training School and home for Nurses in Ashton Street. In 1900 a new Central Home for District Nurses was provided here at 1 Princes Road by funds from the David Lewis Trust.

A recent approach to planning health services in Liverpool echoes the historical roots of district nursing, using localities and neighbourhoods.

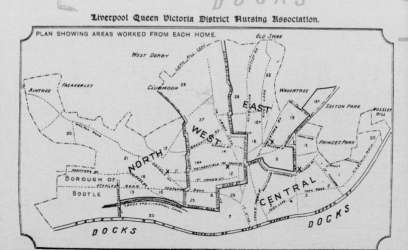

Liverpool Queen Victoria District Nursing Association.

PLAN SHOWING AREAS WORKED FROM EACH HOME.

strict Nursing Association.

William Rathbone IV NB

A district nurse

FROM THE 'JUBILEE CONGRESS OF DISTRICT NURSING 1859–1090'

District Nurses Home NB

Liverpool Medical Institution

The academic quarter

Old Royal Infirmary | Circular Ward

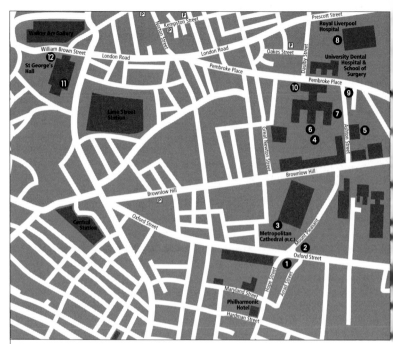

The academic quarter

1. Liverpool Medical Institution
2. Liverpool School of Hygiene (now Centre for Continuing Education)
3. Metropolitan Cathedral of Christ the King
4. University of Liverpool – School of Health Sciences
5. Lock Hospital
6. Old Royal Infirmary School of Medicine Building
7. The Old Royal Liverpool Infirmary
8. The Royal Liverpool University Hospital
9. The Medical School
10. The Liverpool School of Tropical Medicine
11. St George's Plateau, site of the first Liverpool Infirmary
12. St John's Garden

❶ Liverpool Medical Institution

The walk now continues from the Philharmonic Hotel along to where Hope Street meets Oxford Street. Here is the Liverpool Medical Institution.

The Institution's origins go back to 1779, when a group of enlightened doctors formed the Liverpool Medical Library. This provided the medical profession with a collection of books and journals.

One such important medical collection was assembled by the famous Liverpudlian orthopaedic surgeon, Henry Park, of Bold Street. Closely associated with the library was the Liverpool Medical Society, founded in 1833 to promote medical and surgical knowledge. In 1840 the two formally merged to form the Medical Institution, the idea of which had been first published by its founder, Dr John Rutter (1762–1838) in 1833.

Rutter envisaged a centre that would provide for 'every purpose for which it could be required by the profession'. This comment shows that medicine, like other professions during the mid-19th century, was affirming its professional status by developing specialist knowledge and skills which were regularised by examinations and professional codes of conduct issued by establishing bodies.

The building of the Medical Institution, by Clark Rampling in 1836, encapsulates this 'professionalisation' with its dignified curved classical colonnade sweeping around the corner plot. Rampling skillfully assembled a series of spaces which give a relatively small site the appearance of scale and grandeur.

If you enter from the car park to the rear you can see the interior, which is functionally planned with a hall with curved double staircase, a galleried library, lecture theatre, committee and museum rooms. The upper rooms were lit by domed lighting.

In the hall is the memorial tablet to Dr Duncan, President of the Liverpool Medical Society 1836–38, and the Institution's first secretary in 1814.

William Roscoe

The Liverpool Medical Institution was once the site of a bowling green and an inn, where William Roscoe was born in 1753.

William Roscoe (1753–1831) was a polymath, who excelled as a

famous Liverpool scholar, politician, writer, pamphleteer and campaigner against the slave trade. In 1807 Britain finally abolished the slave trade with its colonies, though slavery itself was not abolished by Britain until 1834.

Also closely involved in the campaign against the slave trade were other Liverpudlians, including William Rathbone IV, and Dr James Currie, a distinguished library scholar and physician. There were riots in the streets of Liverpool by merchants who said that this would be the end of the city.

CRO

Some have argued that in many ways the economic decline of Liverpool does date from then. The periodic improvements are generally associated with improvements of trade in time of war and ship building for the forces. Also, the trans-atlantic passenger trade went through a temporary economic boost between about 1890 and 1910.

Also, look for a portrait of Rutter, whose labour and vision was fully realised: the Institution grew in popularity, and distinguished speakers participated in the concept of continuing education for the medical profession.

Most recently the Institute has created a category of membership for non-medical health professionals and has embarked on an ambitious refurbishment programme.

❷ Liverpool School of Hygiene

Opposite the Medical Institution is the former Liverpool School of Hygiene, established in 1897, and now the base for the Centre of Continuing Education Teaching for the University of Liverpool.

The School of Hygiene was the forerunner to the modern University Department of Public Health, now housed in the Whelan Building at the top of Brownlow Hill.

The Sanitary Science Instruction Committee was established jointly by Liverpool City Council and University College Liverpool in 1897. It aimed to provide technical instruction in sanitary science, so that local people could qualify as sanitary inspectors for the local authority.

Closely associated with the Committee's work was the School of Hygiene of the College (later the University). Here medically-qualified students trained for the Diploma in Public Health and medical students were lectured in hygiene.

The School moved to the purpose-built School of Hygiene building at 126 Mount Pleasant in 1919. The ground floor was devoted to a museum of public health. This was used as a teaching aid by medical and veterinary students, trainee health visitors,

nurses and school parties. The museum thus played an important role in the health education of Liverpool.

In 1975 the Sanitary Science Instruction Committee ceased to operate, during the change from old to new public health.

In 1982 the museum's contents went on loan to the National Museums and Galleries on Merseyside.

❸ Metropolitan Cathedral of Christ the King

Directly opposite stands the Roman Catholic Metropolitan Cathedral, built on top of Sir Edwin Lutyen's cathedral crypt, on the site of the Liverpool workhouse.

His cathedral was never completed because of the Second World War. Work began again in the 1960s, to the designs of Sir Frederick Gibberd, and were finished in a very short space of time with very limited finance.

Unfortunately this has led to the need for structural repairs – a not uncommon occurence with buildings constructed in the earlier days of reinforced concrete.

However, the building gives Liverpool a fine example of a mid-20th century ecclesiastical architecture. The centralised church has affectionately been referred to as 'Paddy's Wigwam', in recognition of the Irish links.

❹ University of Liverpool – School of Health Sciences

Along Mount Pleasant, Alfred Waterhouse's Victoria Clock Tower comes into view.

Look across Ashton Street to your left, through the massive archway of the New Arts Building. Here you can glimpse the School of Health Sciences,

The Liverpool Workhouse

On the Metropolitan Cathedral site originally stood the Liverpool Workhouse, one bell from which is now mounted in the Cathedral belfry.

The roots of the workhouse go back to the Liverpool Poor House of 1770. Swelling numbers of urban poor meant a new building was needed. It was constructed on this site in 1824, at a cost of £25,000, and was designed to hold 1,800. The pressure of numbers continued until the site became an incoherent mass of buildings accommodating around 4,000 people – the largest workhouse in the whole of England.

The poor house had an infirmary in which the sick inmates were 'cared for', if you could call it that, by a group of untrained inebriated women. Compounding the appalling lack of care given was a totally inadequate diet and levels of hygiene that were virtually non-existent.

It was again the human efforts of William Rathbone, in consultation with Florence Nightingale, that sought to remedy this frightful situation. A nurse of outstanding ability and commitment was brought, initially at Rathbone's expense, to Liverpool in 1865. Agnes Jones, who was recommended by Florence Nightingale, established the first trained nursing in a workhouse infirmary in England.

Despite difficulties with the administrators over her strict regime and high standards, Agnes ultimately demonstrated that the workhouse infirmary could be run with trained nurses giving excellent patient care together with high hygiene and nutritional standards, at less cost than previously. The personal cost to Agnes was high. She died of typhus in 1866, having noted that she was truly exhausted.

Agnes Jones NB

On her death, Florence wrote to the infirmary nurses asking them not to let this sacrifice be in vain, but to continue her work. Josephine Butler, who had long been aware of the untenable conditions in which the inmates lived, visited the hospital and was impressed with the improvements that Agnes and her staff had brought about.

The original Liverpool Workhouse CRO

The old Medical School extension | The first Old Liverpool Infirmary

housed in the Whelan Building, Johnston Building and Waterhouse's Thompson Yates Building.

The latter has a notable relief sculpture over the entrance, carrying the allegorical figures of physiology and pathology. It is a popular belief that they represent the wives of Professors Sherrington and Boyce. Rupert Boyce was the country's first city bacteriologist and so, with the medical officer of health, constituted a strong team for tackling public health problems in the city.

❺ Lock Hospital

To your right is the Harold Cohen Library, designed by Harold Dod. It opened in 1938 and was recently modernised. This is on the site of the old Lock Hospital for the treatment of venereal disease.

❻ Old Royal Infirmary School of Medicine Building

Along on the left, silhouetted by the incinerator stack of the University's heat and power plant, is the last remaining part of the Royal Infirmary School of Medicine Building.

The Medical School had previously (1834–44) been housed at the Liverpool Royal Institution in Colquitt Street. This building was originally erected in 1844–45, though the remaining section is a later extension of 1873. The school of medicine was absorbed into the new University College, Liverpool as its Medical Faculty in 1873.

Dr Duncan was a physician at the Infirmary 1843–48 (in addition to the other part-time posts he then held).

❼ The Old Royal Liverpool Infirmary

Beside the old medicine building, to the right is the cleared site where the Old Nurses Home of the Liverpool Royal Infirmary stood (built in 1863 and extended in 1891). The cleared site now reveals the pavilion and round wards of Alfred Waterhouse's Royal Liverpool Infirmary.

The building of the Royal Infirmary, which opened in November 1889, was part of the 'enlightened' Liverpudlian response to pressing problems of urbanisation and disease.

There had been two previous infirmaries in Liverpool. By the 1860s, the old Royal Liverpool Infirmary built by Foster in 1824 at Brownlow Hill was totally inadequate. It was ill-equipped to cope with the mounting pressures of population, medical services and medical educational provision. The idea to build a new infirmary of 'inspiration and progress' may have been seeded as early as October 1858 when Florence Nightingale came to Liverpool and presented two papers to a meeting of the National Association for the Promotion of Social Science.

Florence drew widely on her experience of hospitals, and detailed the defects of hospital design and construction, management and practice. She perceived these elements as interdependent, and believed they needed to be combined to develop a 'healthy hospital' that would at least do the sick 'no harm'. (The highly influential professional magazine *The Builder* had already commented (1858) that in most hospitals, cure was by no means a priority, and that patients would have more hope of a cure lying in the open air than in hospital!).

Florence was aware of the connection between poor hospital design and diseases such as sepsis and fever, and of the advanced design and managerial remedies that were to become the principal guidelines for the new Infirmary.

In 1882 the subscribers to the hospital were determined that the old Infirmary be rebuilt, remarking that it was only now fit for their ancestors and should not be tolerated by Liverpudlians.

Alfred Waterhouse (1830–1905), the Liverpool born architect and champion of high Victorian *Gothic,* was a natural choice for the new Infirmary. He had already designed a number of buildings, notably the North Western Hotel on Lime Street and the Prudential Insurance Building in Dale Street. He had considerable experience in hospital design and his habit for spatial planning, massing of buildings and economic consideration was masterly.

The foundation stone was laid by the Earl of Derby on the 28th October 1887, and the building took two years to complete at a final cost of £181,000. Although this was over the estimate of £120,000, it reflected Waterhouse's skill in producing a building of considerable character and utility, on a moderate budget.

The Neo-*Romanesque* and *Gothic* mass and detailing of its exterior gave its frontage a sense of restrained monumentality, yet the real beauty was in the Infirmary's organisation and utility.

There was an innovative heating system using steam pipes and radiators and a modern air circulation system. The design was sensitive to the risks of fire, with the floors having concrete rather than wooden bases. The walls were tiled with glazed coloured brick, allowing for creative designs, which echoed the great Romanesque church interiors of southern France. The overall effect was one of both aesthetic and hygienic attraction, which reaches a visual climax in the hospital chapel, which formed a centrepiece of this Victorian institutional structure, and commented upon the contemporary pre-occupation with the well being of the spirit as well as the body.

The chapel was designed to accommodate 300 people and consisted of a nave, two aisles, a small choir and alter set into a polygonal aspe. It contained a font, pulpit and organ. Its turquoise moulded glazed tiling in abstract floral designs adorned columns, capitals and arcades, which together with a painted ceiling of delicate stars, created an interior of exotic appeal. The windows were restrained in the use of stained glass treatment, save one subsequently inserted, which depicted Florence Nightingale, a Rathbone District Nurse and a Ward Sister. The window was removed at the time of closure in 1978, and taken to the Royal Liverpool University Hospital.

The first patients were admitted to the new Royal Infirmary on the 13th November 1889. The Infirmary had voluntary status but worked closely with the Medical School and, from 1888, the University College, the buildings of which were to Waterhouse's designs.

As demand for hospital services in Liverpool increased, this need was met through a series of extensions to Waterhouse's original design and the creation of a number of new special departments. Prior to the transfer of the Infirmary to state management under the National Health Service 1948, it had been managed by a Board of Trustees who had faced increasing problems in raising funds to meet the operating costs. Capital projects were mainly financed through generous donations and bequests.

Improvements after 1948 were subject to some restriction, as the long term plan was to integrate hospital provision for the city under the United Liverpool Hospitals Board. Lack of space for major extensions at the Infirmary resulted in the decision to build a new hospital in the city centre.

❽ Royal Liverpool University Hospital

The new Royal Liverpool University Hospital at the far end of Ashton Street was designed by Ward Shennan of William Holford and Associates and built between 1966–78.

The last patients left the 'Old Royal' on 17 December 1978. The buildings were boarded up and handed over to Liverpool Health Authority, awaiting a decision on their future. The building was lucky to have escaped the fate of its predecessors and simply lay dormant for 16 years.

Now the Old Royal Liverpool Infirmary has a new future, as development plans are well underway. These include health facilities, teaching and research for the University of Liverpool, and possibly a gallery and museum. Partnership developments involve the laboratories for the University's Department of Pharmacology and Therapeutics and the newly founded Centre for Pharmaco-Economics.

The North West Regional Health Authority has established a Primary Health Care Resource Centre, which will provide the increasing local population with a wide range of facilities which go beyond that of normal general medical practice. The focus will be on education, preventive, diagnostic, curative and rehabilitative activities, which will be delivered by multi-disciplinary teams and a wide range of agencies. Now housed in the centre block is the new clinical skills laboratory, an essential resource to the radical new community orientated medical curriculum in Liverpool.

As such, the Infirmary's new future is clearly in keeping with the sentiments expressed over 130 years ago, when it was determined that an inspirational and progressive Institution of Health should be built for the inhabitants of the City of Liverpool.

❾ The Medical School

To the right at the corner of Ashton Street and Pembroke Place stands the new Medical School. The building was designed by Weightman and Bullen in 1953 and is somewhat undistinguished.

To the left down Pembroke Place, past the old Royal Infirmary, is the Liverpool School of Tropical Medicine.

❿ The Liverpool School of Tropical Medicine

The first such school to be established in this country (and indeed in the world), it was founded in 1898 in response to the call of the Colonial Secretary for the establishment of a training centre for medical officers heading to serve in Britain's colonies.

The necessary funds were raised under the control of a joint committee. This included representatives of University College Liverpool, the Royal Southern Hospital near the docks (which regularly had to deal with malaria, yellow fever and other tropical disease cases coming off the ships), and Liverpool's merchants and shipowners.

The School's first lecturer in Tropical Diseases was Ronald Ross, who in 1902 was awarded the Nobel Prize for Medicine for his research into the origins of malaria.

The School has maintained a worldwide reputation in teaching and research, contributing significantly to the conquest of disease in the developing world. Initially (up to the First World War) this was achieved through expeditions to tropical areas. Later (in the 1920s and 1930s) it was through field stations in these areas, and since

The circular wards in the Old Royal Infirmary

Waterhouse's plan was both inspirational and effective. It consisted of a main administration block with a spinal corridor giving access to a round operating theatre with space for 200 people in the viewing gallery, eight pavilion 'Nightingale Wards', and two blocks of circular wards, with a total of 290 beds and facilities for out-patients.

Nightingale had already recommended that in order to help prevent hospital diseases, certain dimensions for the pavilion wards should be used. She recommended small wards, which were well ventilated and spacious, ideally 16 feet high and not more than 30 feet wide. Window space should not be less than one third of the total wall mass, and the windows should reach from two to three feet from the floor, to one foot from the ceiling. The beds were to be in two rows, with a minimum of five feet of headroom.

Waterhouse was an admirer of the circular ward concept, which he had seen at the Antwerp Civil Hospital, completed in 1884. (In fact, Liverpool actually had its own example of a circular ward that same year, at the Seaforth Cavalry Barracks).

The concept of the round ward was considered to be the invention of Professor John Marshall FRS (1812–1891), and was actively supported during the 1850s and 60s by the editor of 'The Builder', George Godwin FRS. Marshall argued that circular wards enabled light and ventilation from all directions, and extra head and floor space.

All of this was of interest to Nightingale, but she was not convinced that the greater diameter would produce the necessary ventilation. Her concerns may well have arisen from discussion in 'The Builder' in 1882–83 of problems of ventilation at the Antwerp Hospital. During this period enthusiasm for such ward designs began to wain. However the four circular wards were invaluable in providing the required beds numbers with economy of space.

World War Two it has been through collaboration with indigenous centres in the developing countries.

Many current students are drawn from developing countries. This purpose-built building was opened in 1915.

⑩ St George's plateau

Finally, down Pembroke Place and beyond London Road, can be clearly seen the Wellington Column which marks the entrance to the St George's plateau area, and the majestic civic buildings on William Brown Street.

In 1959 a huge barometer stood next to St George's Hall. This was part of the x-ray campaign, initiated by the then Medical Officer of Health for Liverpool, Andrew Semple, to screen Liverpool's population for *tuberculosis* carriers.

The site of Harvey Longsdale Elmes' St George's Hall, a masterpiece of *Greek and Roman* revival architecture, was formerly occupied by Liverpool's first infirmary built in 1748 for 'those in distress from all parts of the nation and Ireland'.

St George's Hall [NB]

Although the infirmary was free to the poor of the town, it was noted by a local historian of the era that entry was restricted, and those who were dying or suffering from fever – ie infectious diseases – were not admitted.

The site was soon to also occupy the Seaman's Hospital of 1752 and, largely due to the efforts of James Currie, the first lunatic asylum in 1792. In 1824 the Infirmary transferred because of the increasing pollution of the Lime Street area of Liverpool.

The 'salubrity' of the old infirmary's situation deteriorated so much that, in 1816, its medical staff were reported as feeling that 'a residence in the infirmary was worse than useless'.

The Infirmary moved to Brownlow Street on whose site now stands Waterhouse's Infirmary buildings.

Not far away in Church Street, a local dispensary was established in 1778 to supply medication to the poor. Dr James Currie, Duncan's uncle, was known to be very active here. In 1806 he initiated a 'house of recovery' for those convalescing from fever. And thus the late 18th century signalled the start of hospital and dispensary care in Liverpool.

⑫ St John's Garden

At the back of St George's Hall is the site of an 18th century Chapel of St Johns, where French Napoleonic soldiers were buried.

The church was an unscholarly and unimpressive piece and was ultimately demolished. Initially the site was earmarked for the new Anglican Cathedral. Fortunately, this never came to fruition for the site would have been competing with that of St George's for prominence.

In its place a memorial garden was laid out in 1904 by the City Surveyor Thomas Shelmerdine. It could almost be described as a garden dedicated to Liverpool worthies. Here we find that William Rathbone, William Gladstone, James Nugent (a child care pioneer), and Thomas Lester (who established the Stanley Hospital and a ragged school for children) amongst others, are remembered.

Medical glossary

Asiatic Cholera
A form of the diarrhoeal disease cholera which took a pandemic (ie world wide) course on a number of occasions in the last century, notably 1832, 1849, 1854 and 1866. It devastated the slum populations in the rapidly growing cities.

Germ theory
A theory that gained acceptance in the late part of the 19th century. It stated that infectious diseases are due to the presence and activity of micro-organisms within the body. The theory gradually replaced the miasma theory of infectious disease (see *Miasma theory*).

Healthy Cities
An initiative promoted by the World Health Organisation from the mid 1980s to encourage partnerships between health and environmental services and the other sectors of everyday life such as housing, and education in the world's cities to improve health. The initiative was based on the recognition that most health is gained and lost in everyday life and that health services as such have a limited, albeit important, role in determining a population's health. It had a resonance with the highly effective Health of Towns Association movement of the mid 1840s which had been inspired by Chadwick's report on the sanitary conditions of the labouring classes in England and which led to powerful Public Health Legislation and city level action.

Homoeopathy
A system of therapeutics founded by Samuel Hahnemann (1755–1843). Diseases are treated by drugs (administered in minute quantities) that would produce in healthy persons symptoms like those of the disease being treated.

Miasma theory
A theory of the 1840s that believed infectious diseases were caused by the bad air from rotting animal and vegetable matter. This was 30 years before the Pasteurs in France came up with the germ theory of disease. Nevertheless, many health interventions resulted from the miasma theory, for example, the ventilation of houses, paving of roads, setting up of municipal water supplies, sewage disposal and street cleansing. All of which had an effect, and were classic examples of doing the right things for the wrong reason.

Ophthalmia
The Victorian term for eye infections.

Primary Health Care
Strictly speaking, the term Primary Health Care includes the prerequisites for health in a population such as adequate shelter and safe and adequate food and water, as well as preventive medical measures and the day to day treatment of the common local illnesses, including that by individuals and their families. The term is often incorrectly shortened to Primary Care and used to describe only the work of doctors, nurses and other professionals.

Secondary Health Care
Typically, medical and social care provided from a community or district hospital.

Tertiary Health Care

Typically, medical and social care provided by specialist units from hospitals which may be some distance from a patient's own district of residence.

Tuberculosis

This is a specific disease caused by the presence and activity of mycobacterium tuberculosis in the body. It can affect almost any tissue or organ in the body, commonly affected are the lungs.

Typhoid

A water or food borne bacterial diarrhoeal disease spread by contamination with human excrement. In epidemic form, it can be a severe disease with a high death rate.

Typhus

A serious epidemic disease with a high death rate caused by a bacterium which is carried by the human louse and spread from person to person by the louse bite. The louse thrives in situations of human squalor.

Architectural glossary

Art Deco
A style in the decorative arts and architecture imported from Paris, and popular between 1925–39, both in Europe and America. Its stylized, angular and modernist forms and details blended mass production techniques with sophistication and exotic design.

Architrave
In classical architecture, the architrave represents the lowest division of the beam. Also refers to the horizontal moulding above a door or window.

Art Nouveau
A dominant style in decorative arts and architecture in Europe between 1895–1910. Its forms and motifs were based on sinuous forms. It was considered 'new' and untainted by historical styles of the past.

Baroque
A style in the decorative arts and architecture during the 17th century and early 18th century. Classical forms and motifs are transformed by exuberance, richness and exaggeration. Dramatic contrasts in light, and complex spatial arrangements make a powerful visual impact.

Doric
The first and the simplist order of classical architecture and decoration.

Gothic
Predominant European style of architecture and decoration from the 12th cenury to the 15th century. It was characterized by the use of the pointed arch, rib vault and flying buttress. This produced buildings that had great height, and were light and airy. The style suited the religious aims of the time. The medieval gothic style was revived in Europe from the late 18th century to the end of the 19th century and was applied to religious and secular buildings and design.

Greek revival
A style in decorative arts and architecture which revived the purity and simplicity of ancient Greek classical forms. Inspired by archaelogical excavations in the mid 18th century. The style found popularity into the early 20th century.

Jacobethan
A mixture of the English style of Elizabethan and Jacobean architecture named after Elizabeth I (1558–1603) and James I (1603–25).

Renaissance
The rebirth in Italy of the principal forms and motifs of ancient classical art and architecture during the 15th century. The style spread throughout Europe during the 16th century.

Romanesque
A style in architecture which dominated European architecture between 800–1100. Characterized by massive rounded-arched, barrel-vaulted ceilings and abstract geometric decorative detailing, it recalled aspects of ancient Roman architecture.

String course
Horizontal moulded band projecting from exterior walls.

Quoins
Corner stones placed at angles of building which are laid in alternate one long, one short arrangement.

Further reading

Ashton, J. and Seymour, H. 1988: *The New Public Health*. Open University Press.

Ashton, J. 1990: 'The Health of Towns and Cities'. *Health Visitor* vol 63, no 12, pp 414–415.

Ashton, J. (ed) 1991: *Healthy Cities*. Open University Press.

Bickerton, TH. 1936: *A Medical History of Liverpool from its Earliest Days to the Year 1920*. Out of print, available through William Brown Library.

Buildings of Liverpool. 1978: Liverpool Heritage Bureau.

Carson, R. 1962: *Silent Spring*. Hamish Hamilton, London.

Chadwick, E. 1842: *Report on an Inquiry into the Sanitary Condition of the Labouring Populations of Great Britain*. Edited with an introduction by MW Flinn. Edinburgh University Press, Facsimile Edition. 1965.

Chave, SPW. 1984: 'Duncan of Liverpool – and some lessons for today'. *Community Medicine* 6: pp61–71.

Frazer, WM. 1947: *Duncan of Liverpool*. Hamish Hamilton.

Hardy, G. 1981: *William Rathbone and the early history of District Nursing*. GW & A Hesketh, Ormskirk.

Hughes, Q. 1993: *Seaport*. Architecture and Townscape in Liverpool. (2nd ed). Blue Coat Press.

Jung, CG. 1963: *Memories, Dreams, Reflections*. Flamingo, published by Fontana Paperbacks.

Lewis, J. 1991: 'The origins and development of public health in the UK' Chapter 2 in **Walter W. Holland et al (eds)**. *Oxford Textbook of Public Health*, 2nd ed, Oxford Univerity Press.

Liverpool Heritage Walk. 1990: Liverpool City Planning Department.

McKeown, T. 1976: *The Role of Medicine – dream, mirage or nemesis?* Nuffield Provincial Hospitals Trust, London.

Pevsner, N. 1969: *The Buildings of England, Lancashire 1: The Industrial and Commercial South*. Penguin.

Procter, M. and Allan, A. (eds). 1991: *Public Health on Merseyside*. A Guide to Local Sources.

Richard, R. 1988: *Death, Dissection and the Destitute*. Pelican.

Shepherd, JA. 1979: *A History of the Liverpool Medical Institution*.

Warren, M. and Francis, H. (eds). 1987: *Recalling the Medical Officer of Health. Writings of Sidney Chave*. King Edwards Hospital Fund for London.

About the authors

Maggi Morris is a lecturer in the Built Environment and Public Health Department of the University of Liverpool. She is a programme co-ordinator for the 150th celebrations of public health in Liverpool.

John Ashton is Regional Director of Public Health and Regional Medicine Officer for the North West of England. He is Professor of Public Health Policy and Strategy at the University of Liverpool.

Notes

Notes

Notes

Notes

Notes

Notes